Carving My Heart
Out of
Splinters

**A Collection of Poetry by
John Hulme**

FIRST EDITION

ISBNs
Paperback: 978-1-80227-503-2
eBook: 978-1-80227-504-9

Dedication

To Marie,
and all the angels who came in her wake.

Table of Contents

For Those

For those who are lost
For those who are wounded
For those who are broken
For those who are shattered
For those who simply feel unseen
For those whose words don't quite feel heard
For those who feel too much
too hard
too deep
too wild
yet still end up feeling they don't feel at all
For those who cry too much
For those whose tears come at all the wrong times
For those who want something sillier
For those who want to breathe more
For those whose feet ache from where they can't go
even when they're not walking
For those who yearn
For those who ache
For those whose love the world can't hold
who end up feeling they don't love enough
For those whose soul is made of crazy, jagged, messed-up things
that still sing like soft green woodland moss
and sea spray
and fine rain on a cotton-cloudy day
and sunshine crumbling on a cool spring breeze
and tide rolling in through the soft crunch of shells
and a hug that rekindles your spirit when you're about to give up

For those who are hurting
and scared
and have to work ten times as hard
to find their way around all the tiny, boxed-in words
they try to tell our hearts to live by
For those who sit behind
windows
and windscreens
and sad little walls
For those who sit out in the rain
For those who hold the rails too tight
For those whose hearts break with the tide
For those whose waves die on the beach
For those whose sunsets drip
like blood from distant dying shores
For those whose fingers clench their fences
For those who splinter
For those who somehow seem to fail
For those who ride in tiny miracles
and on wheels
just wide enough to hide their names in

The Treasure on Fingertips

I saw a miracle,
shining out through tired eyes
and a smile
that could still discover distant stars...

even in me.

I saw a miracle,
spellbound by her fragile,
fearful magic
into a world
whose borders crumbled in a chair...

lighting my Universe with smiles.

Every now and then,
she'd squeeze my fingers,
just to remind me
that holding my hand
would always be the fastest way to freedom.
I watched waves
and stars
and thunderclouds
roll in
across her shoreline...

and I've seen such sunsets in her wake...

but the sky still searches for her fingertips.

The One Thing

Like fragile crystal,
already shattered
and held together with wobbly glue –
shot through
with a kind of shy lightning.
A
very scary,
vulnerable place to be.
I have had about a gazillion people explain to me,
quite knowingly,
where this scared thing comes from
and what it means.
But it's actually something else.
Funny,
when the thing that might just have to curl up and die any
moment –
and take you with it –
is the one thing you're really living for.

Beachcombed and Beyond

I've always loved it,
watching the tide -
always my rolling, go-to place.

Then all of a sudden,
it all fell away,
far beyond windows that looked onto walls...
doorways with guards on,
disclaimers to sign...
pieces of something I don't want to die in,
kicking me
right where I live.

But just with a moment,
a whisper,
a clasp...
you find me again, pull me back in.

The movement...
the texture...
the churn,
so restless, like my own...
so vast
and rippled,
deep
and free...
a touch,
soft enough to rest in…

to dive into a breeze and soak my dreams in…

a space,
vast enough to float my soul in...
wild enough to weave my words in...
a rhythm to set my sea-lit heart by...
a combination,
torchlit through dark
and endless blue...
nature's clockwork,
melting into stories on my tongue...
teasing my passions to speak again.

The fence at the edge of my world will never hold me,
as long as there is a tide.

And what of yours?
Where do your breakers roll in?
Where do you find you?
The real you
that sits in the core of you
and rebuilds itself when anyone wants a piece of you…

If you're in an alley full of dross and there's no way out,
can you find it there?
If you're sitting in an office being talked down to,
can you find it there?
If you're waiting in a blank, little room,
curled up and broken in a blank, little chair
while they prod you with answers and strategies...

staring at someone who just doesn't see,
but who
still tries to tell you what not to be...

If the walls are collapsing around your heart,
can you find the part of your heart that doesn't need walls -
the part that builds bridges in sad, sacred places,
and raises cathedrals
to which your heart alone has the skeleton key?

It's a scary thing to hold in your soul...
scary
and lonely
and painfully free -
rolling ashore on the gallop of waves.

But you know they can't shoot it.
You know they can't jail it.
They can't simply steal it and lock it away.
Whoever "they" might be...
whatever they might say...
however deep their splinters...
however tall their fence...

they can't simply sanction your tide out of churning...
or sanction your heart out of being what it is.

This is the ocean that churns into you.
So crash through those walls when the stone tumbles down,
rip out those splinters

and
scream with the sea
and breathe in what holds you that one time you're free...

'cos this is the fence at the edge of their world
and this is the ocean that churns into you.

Trapeze Practice

I swung on you.
I swung on those threadlights
that spilled out like surf when you smiled.

I was your dancer,
your acrobat,
your tease...
and all the sky was my trapeze.

You cried from a day that caught you
and I cried from a day that fell.

For the Kindness of Dragons

I used to come and stand here,
down by the shore...
right on the line where the waves melted in.

I used to stand proud
against the loud, angry night -
lost like the shooting stars,
churned like the surf...
and beating like,
beating like,
beating like wings.

I used to stand and squeeze my dreams,
here on the promenade,
down by the rails...
watching the tide rolling over the bay.
I once used to pray here -

to pray or to beg...
imploring the spray-woven, thunderous air -

begging for space to phosphoresce...
begging for places to shine...
begging for textures to fill out my heart.

I used to draw here,
with colours that faded when no-one was looking -
with things that sleep in old sea walls,
and come to life when shingle sings...

doodles and scribbles and dragons and things…
doodles and scribbles and dragons…
and me.

I wrote about wingbeats
in vast empty spaces,
and
sketched back the dragons
where dragons were missed -

scooped out of oceans
and feathered with spray...
ignited by things that I wanted to say...
but couldn't find the wings for.

I drew something precious I wanted to be,
if only I'd been deep enough…
if only I'd gone wide enough...
if only these dragons could fill me again...
and the colours wouldn't fade.

I painted the wingbeats that glided over seas
and sketched out the plumage of billow
and fog,
fuelled with fire from shooting stars.

I drew vistas
and coastlines
and planets
and souls...
fuelled with fire from star-shot holes.

I drew wings...
I drew giants...
I drew me...
holding a handful of sea spray...
holding a handful of night...
holding a handful of sunset and fire...
...holding out for the kindness of dragons.

Still Robbing the Stars

The most beautiful thing I saw from here
was a pelican flying over the ocean...
a heron landing on the roof of a getaway car...
a heart finding its feet in the dust...
and a kestrel,
hovering over a phone...
still waiting for the silence to ring...
still waiting for you,
robbing the stars for me.

The most beautiful thing I heard from here
was the first tender stirring of an undiscovered word,
nurtured
in a place where nobody knows I stand...
spilling
from the sound of heavy rain,
just missing the window...
a waterfall,
dropping through a smile
that used to mean everything
and
a small, small voice,
whittled out of
rocks and hills
and things to climb on.

I still need your candle, even now...
even when they douse it from the clouds,
delete you from my files.
You linger illegally in my heart,
still robbing my teardrops...
still calling them stars.

The most beautiful thing I saw from here
was a place I spent the worst part of my life coming home from...
and a notebook
with deep, wet pages,
pinned up to dry in the fine mist between trees...
a pirate ship,
riding the charts of empty inkwells
and still feeling your tides.

The most beautiful thing I saw from here was you,
still setting sail from nowhere...
still setting sail from here...
just to rob those rotten stars
and steal a moon for me.

That One Last Silence in My Clouds

All those twists and turns and tangles -
wrong turns
and stumbles -
looking for a road,
a river...
a trip not taken
to a place all roads now seem to lead:

to a car with no engine,
waiting for midnight
and starlight
and petrol
and me -
watching clouds,
skimming the windscreen
of a long-lost world...
wanting to touch something different but real...
distant but close...
trying to wear a face that doesn't fit -

weave it
and weep it
and breathe the thing free
because this heavy,
floating silence
is deeper than any I have known before -
billowy pillows for a ghost.

Year after year,
I find my way back here,
to an open bedside in the sky,
hoping the Universe will help me get up,
wash my tears and
share my pain
and bleed my spirit clean.

There is,
she told me,
no-one on earth more loved than you.
If only you knew, Son...
if only you knew...
how precious it is to be soft like you are...
and to touch
with your presence
the way that you do.

When I heard these words,
the sobs would come,
the stars would drop
and clouds would shiver like a lifeless weight,
frozen inside my sky...
caught in the fragile stillness of her gaze.

One day,
I told myself,
this weight will lift
and I will float free
to join my friends in the sky:
vast and billowy,

swift like a shoal of cotton-bud sky fish,
or shiny like moon-lit angels,
these clouds
were my ticket to new shores,
to the miracles
that dripped unseen behind every freshly-painted sunset.

I would whisper my heartache to them
as the tide rolled out,
and they would smile back,
whispering soft promises
to the rhythm of the surf
before
drifting off into the night...
and taking the sunsets with them.

And one day indeed,
a new cloud did come,
swooping into my heart
with a brand-new set of wings...
like a night-painted manta ray,
swimming me home across the stars
and changing my perspective
forever.

It rolled
and tumbled
out of endless, haunting eyes,
stuttered
and wept
from thinly-sketched faces at the bus stop,

and hung
like a whipped thing
through the strumming
of a subway guitar.

Sometimes I believe what I feel in its weave.
Sometimes, the billow will shatter -
distant shores
will burn and break
and free those half-sobbed echoes from my throat.
Sometimes,
these high things are more than enough -
these clouds that stop to say hello...
carrying the tears of a lonely Universe
to their deepest,
purest home
beneath the world's wonky RADAR.

Sometimes,
I'm just a dead weight...
standing in a shabby, little,
wordless little place
that feels like it's never gonna let me go -

but sometimes,
I can catch people's breath with my stories
and fill a room with the silence of clouds.

Dark Engine Smoke

Sitting in the car again.
Night.
Summer night.
Warm and still.
Looking out on blackness,
the lapping of gentle water -
nonchalant in the shimmer of streetlights.

Back on the main road, the pubs are spilling out.
Mouths are, too -
big mouths, fuelled on booze and bravado
and the need to scream,
acting like they own the street.
It's the thing you do. Yell out. Fill the space with your noise.
"OLLIE!"
Less a word than a lever - something to turn the sky with:
"OLLIE! OLLIE! OLLIE-OLLIE-OLLIE!"

There are big changes coming.
The world is creaking,
and your mates have just told you where you stand.
So you're shouting
'cos you're angry
and you're in the gang
and you know what the score is
and you're pointing in the right direction.

You're shouting
'cos you're wasted...
and out with your mates -
a streak of lightning in a world of soft clouds.

It's a drunken thing,
walking home in giant shoes
that'll wither by morning -
but
right now,
it all makes sense.

It's a big thing where a child used to live...
screaming at a world that no longer matters
quite the way they said it did...
shouting a word that means nothing,
and filling your bottomless,
burning lungs
with words
that'll mean everything
when the gang gets back together...
sing-signalling your presence over tiny skies.

But it's not my thing.
I think I'll stick with the ripples,
the small tides...
the things that whisper between flashes of wading bird.

There are enough people taking to the street right now.
Enough angry voices.
Enough noise.
Enough dark engines, revving.
There are enough gangs,
glowering down from the skyline.

I want a smaller, deeper flag -
a flag
that sews itself onto my hand
and clings there
like I wrote it myself...
because only your fabric sees my heart
(even now,
when it feels like nobody does).

The streetlamps form an honour guard down the promenade.
It's for people who need to see their way home.
But I'm not going that way.

Echo

I saw your face this morning -
something I needed,
outside of it all.
I reached out,
years too late to feel your skin,
and felt the echoes of your spirit.

These days,
it is the shadows
and empty spaces
that push me forward -
not quite
a ride or a dance or a dream...
just
the last little ticks of nightmare...
falling away.
But here you are,
nestled in blue...
in the surf and the sky
and the morning...
and all of those things I can't do.

Here you are,
filling
this crater of heartbeats
with the echo of yesterday's screams:

"I'm getting better!"

The one damn thing you needed.
The one thing I did, too.
So did the world that forgot you were there...
showing it something,
everywhere.

Sometimes, I'm lost here,
just like you,
slicing my days
with a hot steel blade:

"I'm getting better!"

(from this, from them, from you)

Trying
to shove a kinder,
less merciless truth
into indifferent ears:

"I'm getting better!"

(from this, from them, from stuff you say... from stuff you do)

The only scream
I have left -
and sometimes,
the only scream nobody hears anymore.
A ghost scream,
throwing out my numbers and my codes,
filling
the crater of my heart

with precious bursts of echo,
like that smile:
always the gentlest
of explosions,
your smiles.
Starbursts
in the bear pit...
tiny factories of bonfire,
sat on the edge of a darkening sky
and
blossoming
somewhere between…

I saw you sadder than before.
You saw me deeper in there too.
You hold some part of me
that's still far better in your hands,
haunting
all those happy endings
that came scavenging
in your wake.

The truth is,
I'm more at home in the darkness now,
whittling your echoes into kindling
and lighting our bonfires
with their own kind of peace...
riding out your faces and your loves
and showing the world
(and the lights out of town)
just what they say about me.

I Stand A-Thudding

A summer night. Half-lit stillness where the stars ought to be.
Clouds curl at the edges, billow catches fire, and a small lake of
leftover tidewater sketches
ripples along the edge of the beach.
A pipistrelle hunts over the treeline.
Its random black wings look like holes in the fabric -
but then,
the night hours always were a tease.
A kestrel swoops over the grassland, hovers, shifts suddenly in
the breeze and drops onto a
meal.
An eerie thudding echoes in from the sea.
The lighthouse refuses to reply.
Somebody is planting more wind turbines -
or perhaps flowers.
Giant ones.
Petal sentinels.
Perhaps a welcoming beacon for container ships, as they glide in
from the sacred waters of the
outer galaxy.
Perhaps my imagination has waded out to sea with a giant
hammer.
I promised you a sunset -
and a small token of my humanity.
But then, I promise everyone those things,
without even being sure myself.
I'm afraid I can't give you any more tonight. Not until I figure
out what I have been waiting for all
these years.

It's not in the clouds,
not in their paintwork or their crinkles.
It's not in the breeze,
not what flares up in the chill, makes me catch myself and sway.
It's not in this heart,
not in its rivers, not in my tears.
It's not in the thudding of angry seas.
So why does it haunt my ragged soul? Why is its name written
across my cheek?
Why do I cradle your smile in my hands?
I will stand here forever now...
just a breath away from spaceships and sea monsters.
The full truth of everything that can't be written in books.
A smile.
A kiss.
A long and badly-timed goodbye.
A small child, walking home across the grassy dunes...
knowing that there is no home.
There is only the silence...
the whisper...
the distant thudding of the imagination.
It feels as though it's coming closer.
But it's not.
It's just me, falling away...
much like those last little ghostlets,
chasing the last of that noise-weary tide.
This is my story, my rallying cry, my awkward farewell from the
shoreline.
I crumble.
The sun burns away my voice.
I write my most enduring masterpiece in the stillness of a world
without sentences.

Like When the Stars Pop

You got up,
eased yourself out of a night that felt like a lifetime,
turned
and saw me...
opened up a grin,
pouring your joy
like a sunrise over mountain teeth.

The smile
took me by surprise,
caught my soul in the shockwave,
spilled
an ocean helping of phosphorescent things,
floating like star petals...
a flower,
unfurling the seeds of a new galaxy...
a light with claws,
tender like a laser, like a breeze,
cutting me free
from every piece of rage and tangle...
every little fear...
every little trap.

You showed me then,
deep in a moment
forever etched in pain,
how loved it is...
this thing you held inside your smile.

It broke my heart,
over and over...
made me fragile
in a place I'd barely glimpsed -
a place that seems to own me now.

Back then,
shattered and empty as I was,
I stumbled wearily
and growled,
and the smile died.
I stood there in the coldness
that your flames had left behind,
wanting to
catch you in my arms...
squeeze you
'til the stars popped,
just to hug the spell back...
just to see that smile again.

Instead,
I took up orbit in its glow,
living a life blessed by your forgiveness
and endlessly rekindled
by a colour that still takes the world by surprise,
every time I find that smile.

Somebody Give Me a Mountain

Please,
somebody give me a mountain
and
I'll give you me.
Somebody give me a tide,
lapping a small,
rough shore
that no-one else wants,
like a pebble-fed cat.

Somebody give me a mountain...
a place I can slant,
live at an angle,
watch the soft underbelly of the stars
shattering over lichen-lush rocks.
Just somewhere to wander;
be the thing
that comes out at night,
recharge
in secret lightning...
live a while between sentences.

Then I'll show you
just how deep it goes,
this thing the world can't accommodate.

Somebody told me
a long, long time ago

that I was gonna end up wanting one.
I thought they were being funny,
until the same joke kept showing up
and staring me
square in the roundness of my eyes...
square in the orbits and the wheels,
turning as I write this -
but not joking.

I'm not trying to be greedy.
I'll take one that's broken,
with rusted clockwork
and crazy ridges
that make no sense of the space.
I'll give you things
so intimate
they'll never bounce off...
if you just give me a mountain.

Whalesongery

Rain,
on glass and crinkled iron -
patter to patter to clank.
A trickle streams down windows,
whispering static from blown-out stars,
and a life
written in pebbles
and bubbles
and shells -
and supernova fireworks,
painted through stained-glass rock pools
and moss carpets,
shushing me away from all my tides
and hiding me in trees.
The little room I hid in a while,
played in
like a stowaway -
a lost child,
hiding in a life.
Yeah,
moss carpets,
crunching like piano keys beneath my fingers,
scribbling deep green words
and spores
that scuttle away
from the screens they were typed on -
deep green spores
that leap like dragonflies

into the breeze,
taking the melody with them.
Melancholy,
like the sunset
and the fresh-flame shimmer dance
of autumn leaves...
like
the passion of a stand-up,
outshouting his mic
with his passion,
his rant...
like the whalesong of a dying locomotive,
still sighing
after the rain.
Storm fronts;
performances;
stuff that I do;
the circles I move in;
the shadows I hide in;
the places they meet;
the phrases I hammer on;
pictures in puddles
and things that won't dry;
doors that slam in my face
without looking me in the eye;
doors that creak open and tease me;
doors with thorns and splinters but no handle;
automatic doors,
to which somebody on the other side of the road
always seems to have the controls;

doors that look like dragons,
growing out of trees;
doors that don't look like dragons
(or trees);
sad doors;
happy doors;
"screw it,
step through me
and catch a bus!" doors;
doors that are still too sad to choose;
doors that are tired of smug windows trying to life-coach them;
me,
like this,
right here and right now;
and them,
always in the background,
in my ears
and in my heart;
them when they hear me,
just for a thought,
a heartbeat...
a clap;
me when I speak,
when I mean it,
when I sing;
the echoes of yesterday's gig;
the tears in your eyes when you see what I've lost;
the wheels in my own eyes,
churning out galaxies
every time I look into yours;

the sound of a voice that felt like my own,
surprising itself;
the sound of you, surprising yourself right back;
the whalesong of a dying locomotive,
still pushing on in the silence.

Ghostflies

Now the mountains –
breathless,
fistlike
rising
through a mist of ghostfly eggs and rain…
valleys chopped, rich
and soft
and eerie
with the fog…
screaming with
flame
and bloodstain reds,
and
so much rustier than before…

moss carpets
where the ghostflies play,
splash-knitting streams
and fine green curtains through the woods…
through land that splits
and heaves
like waves…
sprawling lochs
that branch like crystal trees
and shimmer
with those phantom, breezy wings.

Then the cliffs –
immediate,

elephant-faced:
dipping their trunks of rocky barnacle
and mottled green…
red-green…
red-green…
the patchwork flags of ghostfly ink,
declaring their victories
in fire-sword paint
and
browns from a storybook,
written with wingbeat strokes and hope.

Where else
but here
could hope come home?
Curled up in
crumble-brick castles on impossible shores –
curled up with
old stones,
and the blessing
of a deep, fresh rain.

The wetness of swarms that rip through your heart –

how sad a place have you lived in
to weep so painfully over such a weave?
And how much sadder is it now,
to ride your ears
on ghostfly songs
and hear the voice of all things real?

Frayed Out

Running from the all those wayward stars -
hiding
from the acid,
from the flare...
hiding from those broken shards of nightlight,
those spellbound claws
of a jagged moon,
orbiting the beacons...
orbiting the wheels...

the echoes of all those galaxies our hearts once dared to ride,
back when turning was a thing...
back when the Universe was just a touch and a whisper away...

and you were the shores.

I am a smokestack now -
a deep-sea chimney,
melting gemstones
stolen
from that sparkle on the tide.

I feed on your warmth as my core grows cold.
I live like a thing made of bonfire and wing,
frayed and torn
and
lifted
by all those harsh and killing things
the world whittled in my eyes -

looking always to you,
the champion of paper aeroplanes,
to stitch back the thermals and weave back my sky.

I'm a deep-sea chimney,
billowing stars,
watching them float into cloudlight and space fish...
watching our stories get eaten,
tangled in margins,
crumpled like shells...
watching an army of throwaway doodles
blot out your smile,
gun down my hope
and then despise me for losing your kindness.

I am an echo of starships and you,
mourning a love that came out to play...
a love that weeps stars when my wings start to fray.

Safeword

We covered so much floor with all those words,
still with our mountains locked beyond the walls.

I wish
there had been a safe word
for those little sessions in the kitchen -
those slow mosquito raids
on my soul,
always to the clink of glasses
and the stale stench of
one
too
many.

I wish there'd been a
get-out clause...
and a mountain,
made of sunrise,
sunset,
ripple blue
and ocean...
waiting to let me walk it off.

The Fence They Shoot Hopes on

They say it's the hope, don't they?

They say it's the hope that kills you -
the ragged things you just can't hold
for fear
that glass will shatter...
cathedral windows in your palms...
stained-glass things
that pull away with paint-flecked wings...
shell-shocked
from the slamming of a few too many doors.

They say it's the hope that kills you,
here in this windy, walking place
that pulls you in circles
and alleys
and knots,
'til you're caught in a snare
that you can't ever share -

here, by the fence at the end of the world,
wrapping your hands
in the rags of old flags,
squeezing the love out of every last thorn...
moments of rust
and old barbed wire
and pages waiting to be torn...
or scribbled over.

They say it's a vision of unseen shores,
weeping
between wounded fingers.

They say it's you,
climbing the wall at the end of the world -
the fragile child of armistice,
holding the rhythms of mine-peppered air...
trying to find the peace in despair.

They say it's you,
keeping a truce that broke in the night
and
holding the world with a small, sacred light.

They say it's you,
carrying a pack of torn pages
and spent ammunition -
holding up the silence,
one
watchtower
at
a
time...
while armistice shivers inside you,
dreaming the stars out through hair-trigger guns.

One last stand
and one last kiss -
we need a better peace than this.

The Home that Found Me

Was it the line of dragon spine
curving like a serpent through the hills?
Was it the wetsong,
chorused over stones?
Or a head,
leaning on a bathroom wall,
waiting for love
to reach through cold things
and tears?
Was it the moss,
thick like a rug over ancient roots?
Or a heart
that shivered in a few too many streetlights,
waiting for night
to call me home?
Was it the cloud,
hanging over mountainside
and stoic rock?
(drifting like kindnesses and smiles)
Or was it the tide,
painted
in phosphorescence
for
that one wild party through the moonbeams?
The rhythm of something
as endless as the hug
that saved my heart -
only to discover that once would never be enough.

Or was it a river,
pawing,
hound-like,
at my door?
I struggle to ask for help these days,
having seen
too often
what this world thinks help looks like.
So is this the home that found me?
Cloud
and rain
and rich, damp moss
and walls where the tears come rolling home.

Window Catch

I watched you from a scary place...
watched the way you looked at me,
picked my face
out of all those windows...
all those rooms you didn't belong in.

I watched the way you caught my smile,
teased the air between us
like a dance.

I thought of all those times I did the same.
Sometimes I did these things for ghosts...
for things that were barely even there,
yet
subtly hanging everywhere...

Sometimes I did these things for life...
for people...
people who were there just a little too much...
people who shine here so damn much,
they still haunt me...
just like ghosts do...
just like hope.

Maybe you've been waiting for some hope of your own.
Maybe it's the window looking back at you now,
spinning and skating,
spinning on teardrops,

spinning on ice...
pirouetting itself through all those eyes...
all those precious,
night-lit eyes
who saw you through pictures of raindrop and glass -
all those eyes you tried to catch.

Maybe there's something else out there,
waiting for you
even now
in skies you thought you were too tired to stand under anymore.

Either way, I think it sees.
I think it knows you,
window girl.

I think it's been reading your name out of stars,
burning their warmth into cold, empty glass -
hoping for all the things you've ever been
or seen...
making those windows come alive...
beyond
and better
and a billion things besides -
for the world where you catch things, deep in those eyes.

Things I Learned from Ballast

I can't write fast enough to light the stars,
or bake enough galaxies
for the recipe.

I'd happily weave an ocean from the lamps,
and set it free
to stretch and swell across the night -
a skeletal thing,
fashioned from plankton glow,
floating where water ought to be.

But I don't have the water anymore.
I have nothing now but lights,
making fire
where giants and legends used to swim...
stirring the core back,
deep into space,
and cooking my Universe anew,
stitch by tiny, gentle stitch,
spark by gentle, loving spark...
simmering a tide with fingers,
stretching out from the lights of a distant place...
teasing me
with the touch of something still undrawn.

I know from these charts that the ocean is ours...
but I can't write fast enough to light the stars.
Even without the water...
even without the soul...

it still has enough of a rhythm
to stitch back all those pieces
that others have steadily chipped away
in their attempts to sensibly redefine me.

But then along comes you,
rebuilding the treasures I least expect...
rinsing my heart,
wave after wave,
with a spirit I didn't see coming.
Perhaps you know what you are.
Perhaps you don't.
Perhaps you lean on rusted railings,
just like me,
watching for ships that never come in;
stowing away
in ballast tanks,
riding half-empty container vessels
with a small fellowship of displaced sea things,
sucked up to make up the weight.

Cargoes of convenience,
they call us -
hobo stars -
riding blind through the strangest of seas
and
waiting to land somewhere inconvenient,
unlit
and hungry for the undrawable.

I know from your heart that this ocean is ours...
but I can't write fast enough to light the stars.

Harsh Paint

Sometimes,
simply standing was enough -
simply standing in a place
where everything grinds and grates.

Every now and then,
you'd find yourself fighting my monsters again,
wrestling
teeth and tentacles
for custody of my arms -
the hand that scratched and the arm that bled.

They'd paint the air, these scratches,
right across the sky,
like vapour trails.
They'd leave the world tattooed on skin,
still growling
and snarling
and pulling me down -
harsh stars.

They were yours once -
yours to watch
and fuss over,
you being the one place I couldn't hide my pollution from.

You hated them,
hated seeing me make them,
even made me weep for hurting you -
the one weapon you had left,
your wounded disapproval,
handwritten in the clouds.

But you knew the skies I ached for...
and you knew,
better than anyone,
that scratches were as close as I could get -
the vapour trails
of tiny fingernail flights.

So you owned the days when I made them...
sat and held me through them
and told me stories of a love
big enough to scrape me free
from all those jet wounds in my soul.

Weeping with the Jellyfish

Phantoms.
As darkly massive as they are,
they slide with the spirits in this mist.
Giant bell-shapes,
resting like deep sea jellyfish –

the grey, solid monsters
of a ghost ocean…
creatures of wet weave,
at home in the drift of cloud,
the trawl of wetness over brown sponge,
green, flecked with orange…
and milky light from moorland pools.

And
when they solidify,
their magnificence overwhelms what remains of my soul –
rocks like rockets from the ocean floor,
jabbing jagged at the sky,
yet somehow close enough to touch…
to sweep me up with the star-bound exodus of stone.

What looks down…
What glares from the deep grey billow in its eye…
What rips all those tears clear out of the sky,
tumbling
down leviathan pleats...
guiding me home

in spite of all timetables...
guiding me to home to this rampant elsewhere...

A wetness to dissolve in -
to lose myself
in the communion of
all things washed away
and all things coming up for air,
unzipping stars
and forests
from the ocean you left on the soles of my shoes...
from feet
that would never walk dry again.

I am a scream here –
a scream as wild as beauty gets.

The bus pulls into the land of houses -
my home,
through no fault of the brick -
and the real wilderness begins;
where stone is just stone
and tears are just gutter food.

Take Your Pills and Hide Your Eyes

A hijacked life...
a twisted plot...
a knocked-down door that makes no sense...
and a woman,
counting her heartbeats on the street.
A girl abducted years ago,
dying for the cameras -
a soiled tarpaulin,
wiping off a childhood long since stolen by the sex trade.
Is this a poem for the screen?
I don't have the scribbles
and I don't have the heart.
So
is this where love
comes home to die?
Too wizened to smile -
the way you did,
determined as you were
not to kill me with your dying
or soil my kindness with your pain.
But just like you,
hers was a kindness
mocked and abused -
in her case,
trafficked and
relentlessly used.
Yet still such beauty in her eyes.
As broken,

unseen
and
alone
as they are,
there's still such beauty in her eyes.
She'll die
by the morning,
bequeathing her pain to a broadcast,
tragic and flickering,
dancing for strangers in sad little rooms,
igniting the damage in their own lives.
They'll take off their masks
and they'll weep when they see
so much beauty...
so much beauty in her eyes.
So many lives have been stolen.
So many childhoods have cried.
Silence is bleeding
all over the world...
and still such beauty in her eyes.
My voice...
Her voice...
Your voice now...
The voice we lose...
The voice we kill...
Get on the bus
and take your pill...
Look in the camera,
take your pill...
Lie on the bed
and take your pill...

Shut down your heart
and take your pill...
and still such beauty in her eyes.
The one big thing we still don't say.
I'm sorry I failed you
by being so small...
with one big secret,
cupped and cradled in my hands...
and one more taste I can't smile back...
and still such beauty...
still such beauty...
still such beauty in this land behind our eyes.

Flagweavery

There is a flag
woven into your heart.
There is a flag
whose colours were born
behind every conversation that ever left you
catching your breath,
choking back tears that caught you by surprise.
There is a flag
whose symbolism
is sitting on your shoulder
beneath the sky you can't turn away from,
the clouds whose stories you're aching to tell
and the vapour trails of flights
only your imagination can catch.
There is a flag
whose textures have never looked more heroic
than when the threads are worn
and frayed
and close to hopeless
in a land where sewing is outlawed
and tapestries are only for the rich and the powerful.
There is a flag
you can't fight for
without having wiped it over your sweaty face,
wept into it
and felt it die a little in your shivering hands.
There is a flag
that stands in the face of disapproval

and water cannons
and bullets
and the screams of people with bigger placards
and catchier slogans...
There is a flag whose sentences are soft
and beautiful
and as elegant as the sunset,
simply because you hold it like the sunlight in your eyes...
and you don't turn away.

Opening the Trunk Roads

I wander a maze of endless roads,
most of which seem to lead me right back to the empty room I started
from.

I remember those massive, wild things,
lifting my story with their presence,
back when my world showed me too many walls,
and all I really wanted was to break them down.

The screen shimmers a little, and the person sitting next to me is
holding my hand with fragile
fingers as we watch, reminding me of migrations we took together,
in secret places they don't
make documentaries about...

Did you stand guard over my body in another life?
Did you raise your voice to the evening sky and bounce your
songs of mourning into the
distance?
Did you run your trunk over my dead bones?
Did you pour your secret, weeping whispers over my spirit?
As I lay there,
not wanting to leave your devotion behind,
was it your song that carried me back to all those ancient paths?
Was it your song that brought to life the patterns I had made
across your sacred highways?
And was that approval I felt across my cheek,
or just soft rain?

Is it your song that haunts me now?
Is it your song that keeps me from stumbling, in this broken
world where all roads keep us
apart?
It feels at times as though my life barely belongs here, in this
body, in these streets, behind
these windows...
yet one distant song continues to keep me strong.
Did you bless my bones once, so I would know, even here, that
I still have friends in the herd?
And will it still be worth it, when our worlds come back together?
If so,
then keep the roads open for me,
trumpet my regards to all the other lost souls who wander here,
and walk a little by my side -
for there are worse ways to live,
and far worse ways for a song to die.

A Delicate Rewrite

Each day, Sketchy rubbed out a few more of her colours.

I knew this,
way before the story broke.
I knew this
because I died a little too,
every time she came back home,
turned her key in the door
and flipped my heart.

Each day, as people tore her off a strip,
took her down a peg
and gradually hacked away at her fragile foundations,
a little more of her shading began to unravel,
unstitch
and generally discombobulate.

I knew this
because I cried too,
every time she shut the closet door
and curled up
in my shadows.

Sketchy never said the right thing,
or did what other people thought she was supposed to do.
They said so on all the forms
and in all the classrooms
and the kitchens
and shops

and offices
and garages –
and all the proper places
where all the proper colours were made
and then tested
to make sure they stood up to argument.

Sketchy never seemed to achieve anything
or win anything
(besides scoldings
and sneers
and the superior smirks
of people who loved having soft targets
to laugh at).
The only thing she ever seemed to do
was slink away
and disappear.

What nobody else noticed,
outside
the lamplight
that held us tight against the night,
was just how completely she was vanishing.
They couldn't see the soft clockwork eroding inside her,
the small dead cogs
in my hallway...
They couldn't see the unwanted colours dissolving in her tears,
drowning in mine.

Without even realising it,
Sketchy was becoming quietly brilliant at the strange art of
self-erasure.
With slow,
deliberate strokes,
she was
rubbing away the very essence of her soul –
until only a few stubborn strokes of core Sketchy remained,
floating in a kind of aimless abandon,
like shells caught in the tide.

I used to love the tide back then -
the last place I could stand
with any semblance of shelter
to
cuddle my nightlit sister through the storm
and
fill all the cracks with surf and splash
and wave beats,
drummed from the fingers of faraway shores.

Those were the shores
on which Sketchy
revived,
rekindled in her driftwood mask,
stumbling home
through the sad world that lived by default behind Sketchy's
eyes,
where everything felt lost and unwanted until it had been given
a name…

but somehow,
nothing seemed right
until all the names and labels had peeled away.

Sailing home
through the downtrodden oceans in my soul,
Sketchy began to chart the stars
I'd missed -
and to navigate by them.
That's when she knew
she wasn't erasing anymore.
She was painting herself...
weaving herself home through new currents...
charting her way to new shores,
where her shaky voice might, at last, have real stories to tell.

If only she could find the words.
If only she could stir mine,
and build some moonlight in this vast
but faithless
little heart.

If only we both hadn't spent so long
fighting fires between the lines
on which other people wrote their meanings.
If only there was a voice for things unspoken.

There were still so many subtle terrors in this place of churn and
brushstrokes.

But at least now,
when people meet Sketchy,
or me,
or one of the faces we dance in
(somewhere lost between the two),
even if they don't quite understand the colours,
even if they don't believe the shell patterns in our eyes,
they're never left in any doubt
that there are still masterpieces waiting, somewhere out beyond
our shoreline.

Where the Stars Should Be

You're not
what they tell you your age is.
You're not
what they tell you your gender should be.
You're not
what they think of the way that you live
or the things that you do
or the things that you don't.
You're not
what your bank balance
tells you you're worth.
You're not what they tell you,
what side of the street...
You're not just the place that they tell you to stand.
They'll label you,
they'll box you in;
they'll sit your soul in small, sad rooms;
they'll prod you
and poke you
and weaponise you;
they'll watch us tear ourselves to shreds;
they'll
point their lies across the street,
lighting those
empty little,
nasty little fires
between the things we never were.

They'll leave you to wither
in
smallness,
put the lie of your life on a leaflet,
signed
with a punchline,
a big phoney smile
and a picture of someone you know is not you,
woven for speeches
and empty applause…
filling
the airless, broken space
where
the truth of your spirit is desperate to breathe…
where your vast inside
could swim and glide.

You're not the small,
sad thing
they painted here,
with nothing but burning cars
and missiles
to draw yourself home with.
You're a lost thing,
stumbling along
on its way to so much,
so much more,
being sold the lie
of what a warrior you are
by small voices
that would rather see a sword in your hand

than a new word
stretching over burning cars
and broken streets
and small things
dying
where the stars should be.

Daring

Where did she find that awesome voice?
Shining as it is,
cascading
down her flouncy, bouncy hair
like a chortle-weave waterfall…

How did she find that magical,
magnetospherical
slice of speaksong?
The voice I need so much it hurts…
the voice I need,
I need tonight.

And how did she make it look so easy?
If I could find a voice like that,
turning me
up a notch,
making me giggly with release –
like stars unfolding
in the promise of her touch…
If I could be
the chatty little grinning thing
who sits at the edge of the table
and curls like a puppy
on firm,
gentle thighs –
telling herself she'll be treasured tonight…

Much like those cracks in her smile
and her wings,
those thighs are
far less brave than they might seem,
for all the symbolism on that belt buckle.

She's more like that fray on the edge of her shorts…
an end of something,
hoping not to tumble out and disappear
before he
says something funny again,
before he laces the fear between giggles with something like
kindness.

I thought I'd caught all those orbits,
once upon a night –
but now she has it –
she has the voice,
putting all manner of cosmic wheels on hold
by daring to believe it.

Untreatably Me

I've hit a place where everything dies.
Or maybe I'm simply dying for a hand,
holding mine
like it's really there...
and walking me free
just like
someone real I used to be
but never quite got the hang of.

But what I don't want...
What I don't want is your help.

I don't want any more of your tests
and your sad,
scary waiting rooms
and your scanning, seeing, sorting machines,
running on clockwork
and fairy tales.

I don't want a thousand ways to label me away.
I don't want a number or a code
or a class
to teach me out of darkness.
I wither in your heartless light
and on your silly bloody charts.
I don't want your pills
or your sick notes
or your half-hearted dose of talk therapy

with a diagram thrown in.
I don't want your cold,
soulless rooms
and your smug, dead eyes,
looking for clever,
funny ways
to be condescending
about all the things I'm doing wrong
and all the things I have to change
to be
what I never wanted to be
and what nobody who ever felt the truth of me
ever wanted to see.

I don't want your words
or your answers
or your glowing testimonials,
because
all the love that died on me
apparently shone on you.
I just want to get up
without this banshee dying in my soul
or these cataract windows
taunting the view from my heart
or
a million things to scare me
out of breathing…

I just want me back...
even now,
when all those poems
and stories
and stars
have died with the one set of eyes who knew...
and the one clear light that's screaming too.

Not Like You Do

I have had stranger friends before.
I have had friends
made out of float light -
the rub-woven
phosphorescence
between all those tides I watched;
echoes,
dropped from the sunset.

I have had friends who see me
through the nuts and bolts and clichés
of how this world insists I should be mapped.

But they don't really rescue -
not like you do.

I have had friends
made out of candles -
little
tealight
bonfires,
pretending I still have mountains
to walk through;
pretending they'll be here when nothing else will.

But they don't really rescue -
not like you do.

I have had friends
made out of drums and angry songs...
made out of
desperate,
seething,
half-seen words
or sometimes,
just rain on a window -
tears
from those holes in the sky,
drilling their hope through the edge of my life.

But they don't really rescue -
not like you do.

I have friends
who ache to see me clothed in light...
but
I have a houseboat in this dark place now,
and a heart
too used to the ripple and the roll.

It feels emptier now than I'd like it,
but the stars don't get it -
not like you do.

Craving the Love that Catches Me Out in Space

where do i go
when i'm lovable?
when i'm lost and soft
like angels playing in the rain...
and hungry
like your fingers feel
on glass.
...so, if i'm rain...
i guess i must be billions...
gazillions...
a holocaust in a puddle,
waiting
like wet, galactic dog,
spinning those drenched,
those newborn stars...
and pleading with you,
rusted listener though you are,
to hear the oceans falling home...
and simply,
simply let me go.
i need the freedom...
crave the space...
but where do i go
when I'm lovable?
when i'm gentle and damp
like demons redeeming themselves in rain...
and angry
like my legs once felt

on grass...
where i waited for you.
i am a sunbeam,
a candle...
a flame gone crazy
and gone out.
i am a slate,
washed clean with words
that only the rain will ever understand.

Now You're a Staircase

Is that you I'm looking for?
Even though I know you're not there. You were never there -
my invisible playmate, hand to hold, ear to listen...
hole to fall into.

You were the hole torn into carpet
and silly,
half-written stories.
You were the hole that kept me alive,
kept me
breathing
when the life caught in my throat.
You were the other part,
the bit that made me...
me.

You were the blue thing,
smiling round the moon that night.
You were the one night that stands out in my heart,
when suddenly everything felt like a dance...
and it didn't matter if I tore out the pages.

You were the blue thing,
lighting the surf like a match
and burning my soul across the water.
You were my ripple wake,
my sunset reflected out to sea...
anywhere I wanted to go.

Maybe you're just driftwood,
like a doll.
Maybe you're just something else I lost.

But I feel you now,
charging the wheels in my engines,
sparking
the galaxies,
lighting me home...
and winding me down
through
all these stars...
like a staircase
whittled out of cosmic dust and earthly fear.

Music Box Lights

Starfall on helter-skelter moonbeams -
snapping the handcuffs
of a tiny life,
made smaller by every drop of rain
that fails to land.
A dry place,
thanks to stupid things and lies.
Streetlamp fire on rippling tidewater -
burning you free
like a cold smoke...
like a mist...
like a rolling, prowling, light-giving thing...
stalking a world
where everything seems to claim your name...
telling you who you need to be,
telling you how you need to think,
telling you all the things you're not...
and all those tunes your heart won't play
however many times you try to wind up the rusted little music
box in your heart.
Yes,
that was the day they impounded the flame -
the day they imposed sanctions on kindness,
banned it from our eyes
and sold it off for firewood.
That was the day -
'cos none of them care that you feel this way.
That was the day

they pulled the shutters down
over all our windows,
stopped us looking out
on the things strong enough to make us cry.
That was the day,
scrawled like fingers on a bully's blackboard,
when the world as I loved it
started
to
die.
That was the day I took a hammer to a rusty music box.

The Things in Wetness

Sometimes the wetness is a whispering thing,
a teasing thing,
like an arm, not quite ready to reach out for your shoulder.
Then the skies start to unzip,
texturing things that can no longer hide what they are.
Ripples and rolls turn to galloping things,
and the spirit inside you starts drumming again,
like an orphan thing,
a running thing –
a thing that never quite learned how to sing.
The dance holds you in its dripping hands,
reminding you
that even the fallenest stars can run on fun…
on pillows and fabrics,
colours and fires…
and a part of you that never has to justify the wrong, crazy
choices
in the wrong, crazy world.

Runaway

Show me a nowhere
so I can run away there.
Show me a nothing,
empty
like the creases in a tarpaulin sky.
Show me a nowhere,
empty like the pleating
in a curtain
or
a skirt
or a fluffy-woven,
mossy-woven
tapestry of tree...
a ripple,
running down a window
as it
whistles in the rain...
rolling like a broken vessel,
dying in the misty distance,
somewhere
out at sea...
remembering how I used to be me.
Show me a nowhere,
somewhere that's lost
and
achingly bare...
and
I will run away there,

spilling my damages everywhere.
Show me a nowhere,
a billion more
steps from standing out here...
and
I will run away there,
spilling my damages everywhere.
Drowning my soul
in a bucket of
nowhere,
somewhere that's lost
and
achingly bare...
I will run away there.
I will run away there.
I will run away there...
spilling my damages everywhere...
spilling the rain
and the stars
and the glass...
looking through lenses that melted me in...
running from pictures
and passwords
and names
and a life that aches for something real
when even our treasures get
forged
into games.
So show me a nowhere,
a billion more poems
from standing out here...

and
I will run away there,
spilling my damages everywhere...
I will run away there.
I will run away there.
I will run away there...
spilling my damages everywhere.

Cascade in Red Pants

*I was standing on the edge of a mountain footpath, hugging visions
of someone who danced
with me once. She danced with people who knew me more than a
few times along the way, and
she left her footprints on places they're not allowed to talk about anymore.
I was standing in that blue-lit half-clouded place between sunshine
and rain, trying to let go of
something I had carried with me forever. Then, without a word,
she stepped out of me and
danced…*

Sunlight on the mountain,
hoping the light rising from my soul will meet it -
a small fountain meeting a river,
shedding its broken parts one more time,
like a rusty, jangling robot
in my head,
aching for healing from a wound that will always be invisible.

I'm wearing my crinkly blue raincoat like a skirt,
dancing a little in the turn of tears,
just
as a lost planet
peeks out of the cloud,
spills its cargo of angry sparks -
one creaky clockwork saluting another.

You'd consider me wanton if you saw me now,
with

nothing under this coat
but an old red sweatshirt
and those silly, frilly scarlet pants -
the ones I wore to practise my pirouettes in your mirror.

But after hiding in all those rotten doorways,
curling up
in all that rotten timber...
after shoving back all those stained coins and clickbait chip
paper...
this,
at last,
is *my* burlesque,
applauding my thighs with high country wetness and breeze.
This is *my* ballet,
one last time
before somebody else comes to steal it.

They stole a billion sleeve notes on the road I took to get here.
But this book,
however torn and tawdry you think the dance,
the outfit,
the slow corkscrew finish as my behind drills into soft, damp moss,
my legs cross
and my broken robot brain feels whole again
in the echo of a gazillion moments
where love pinched me inappropriately from a dark place -
this is my book.

This is where I stop caring,
and the rest of me cascades.

Such a Long Way Down the Road

And then there was my heart,
my words,
my little bridges through the stars,
the streetlamps
and the surf,
rolling in static like a hungry radio...
and then there was my
smile,
bigger than I ever could have hoped
after all those disappointments
on the broken kitchen floor -
that smile
you'd break the speed limit for.
Such a long way down the road.
And then there were my tears,
shockingly vast
in the eyes of your ships...
breaking me loose.
Droplets of poetry and pain,
and one last concrete,
rampway
subway
of a hill to roll me down...
back to a puddle with stars inside...
back to an ocean
worthy of tears.
And all
such a long way down the road.

But
now I'm the poem you don't read.
Now I'm the voice that can't stand up,
be loud,
be proud,
be heard.
Now I'm the dewdrop who drifts away...
whose ticket
never made it through the day.
Now I'm the one last starship on the page...
doodled with stardust
and spillage
and flares...
kicking stones and asteroids,
only a twisted light year down the road.

Stripped Down to the Me

One of those nights when there is quite simply nothing - no place to
call, no name in my contact
list that fits the dark shadow where the midnight jigsaw pieces have
fallen out...
nowhere to go and hide between all the turned-off lives and the
stars.
There's just me...
which is simply not enough to deal with being me.

Struggling.
In ways I can't easily talk about.
In ways I can barely breathe.
Struggling.
Curling up.
Crumbling.
Losing the will.
Losing my heart,
my words,
my warm little candle,
held against the chill.
Losing.
Just losing,
losing me.
Scared I played me all the way wrong.
Just losing.
Just lost.
Just broken
and cold.

Just empty.
Just struggling.
Alone.
Hard to connect when we're so out of sync.
You really can't hear
what I say,
what I am,
what I do.
I try to be me
in a world that's too...
you -
and I'm struggling.
Been here before...
can't take anymore.
'cos I'm...
struggling.
Round and round in circles,
in circles you can't read.
I don't wanna quit.
I don't wanna stop.
I don't wanna drop without a fight...
at the very least,
a rescue light.
But I'm nothing,
I'm losing,
I'm struggling.
I'm gone.
Behind a window.
Behind a wall.
Behind a life that never worked...
pretending I was special...

pretending I was gliding...
pretending I was in these words,
these stories...
these poems, where my heart met yours.
These stories...
these lies.
I'm screaming tonight,
screaming inside.

I'm waiting for a place where the air is somewhere above frozen...
where the heart is
somewhere above me. And I'm struggling... I'm lost.
And I'm frightened of the silence... lovers though we've often been...
and I'm frightened even more to share.
Frightened of what the page will see.
Frightened of what the page will say.

Moss-Lit

A million...
a billion...
you,
me...
a star, stuck in a snow globe
or a pinball machine.
All those homeless vulnerabilities,
waiting to share themselves,
to sprint again,
feel the crumble as the embers swarm around our heels...
I lost myself,
burned away
and found you waiting
on the fluffy far side of my palm,
food for giant, wordless ferns
who hear me still.
The world stole all these things a thousand times,
and still you listened
with the friendless fellowship of weavery and fronds.
I run my hand across a wall,
cutting my kindling...
lighting my skies…

Sometimes the smallest little rug of rich, damp, living texture is enough,
like a small star in brickwork,
lit, in one of those giggly, cosmic ironies, not by fire but by rain…

A Page Between Raindrops

Sometimes, I was telling someone the other day, clouds come down from the sky to play.
Sometimes, the clouds drop low enough to cuddle the mountains.

You can see them chasing each other between the ridges, wrapping themselves around the
peaks; curling and stretching in foggy games of hide and seek.

Water, made playful in the presence of rock, makes eerie giants out of wet cloaks... turning
stone into phantom things that disappear in a flurry of billow.

Massive, glowering things become a playground - a storybook for faceless ghosts.

And when you trust the churning of imagination behind your eyes, you start soaking up the rain and the streams, feeling the lie of waterproofing and the truth of cheerfully sodden feet.

You start seeing the pages open when the clouds come down.

You can see how spore gills weave music into a fungus, how the softness of green re-invents
kindness on a mossy stone.

It helps sometimes if you're on your own, without other people's voices to shoot you down or tell you how they have thought the same things better.

Trust me - if you truly see such miraculous things in the deep, wet places where playful clouds
have chased each other, the smarter voices haven't come close.

Not to you.

Not to your bottomless heart, with its heaving ocean full of poems.

Not to the soft rain on your lips, looking for dry places to save.

Not to the brave, white waterfall snakes who dive down the mountainsides, dying over and over, just to remind you of something that meaner voices should have killed a million times already.

You're a lingering magician between raindrops and snakes, wearing crazy-coloured socks that
leak dye over the rivers.
You're a cleft in the mountains, weeping white snakes all the way down to the sea.
You're an idea that ran away to the circus and found it in a puddle.
You're a poem that slipped face first in the mud.

You're all the wrong choices and all the wrong answers, finding your way to something the world will never be ready for.

But you're bleeding it anyway, from the waterfalls in your eyes and the ink in your notebook and those crazy dyes in your socks, breathing the fire of soft things into fungal gills and kind green moss.

You're the thing that walks between raindrops, even when the mean things sweep your legs from under you, remembering things they should have killed a million times already.

What I Mean About Bears

So when I came here,
I brought a bear along...

as you do.

A big, floppy-fluffy teddy bear with big shiny eyes.

Kind of like a mascot, y'know?

Something silly.
Something furry.
Something that hugs
and squishes
and makes those crazy goo-goo cuddle eyes
with eyes that ought not to see me there at all.

Something that holds me when nothing else will...

and reminds me
how often I have needed
just that
to get me through impossible places.

So now I'm here,
in another impossible place,
far beyond all the streets that used to swallow me -

a place made of wetness
and stone
and sun
and the colours that ballet and pole dance between them.

Now I'm here...

offering hugs
to sunsets,
floppy, pebble-slapping tides,
wall moss,
heron-chasing river songs,
cloud-eating mountains,
sunset-nibbling swans...

and people who know what I mean about bears.

Something Otherwise Entirely

It wasn't a call for a rally.
It wasn't a call for a crowd.

It wasn't a certainty,
sparring with yours.

I wasn't creating a cause.

I wasn't debating the content of test tubes
or pulling the point off your needles,
fired
into angry,
vibe-fed,
hungry souls.

It wasn't a rant at the science.

It wasn't a scream at the scandals,
trailing like smoke
from burning cars and barricades.

It wasn't a song about who we should praise
and who we should scorn
or who gets the kudos for speaking their truth -

who stays lost and who gets born.

It wasn't a thing you could rally.

It wasn't a cause you could chant.

It wasn't your flags and your trucks and your borders.

It wasn't your oil and your trees and your driftnets.

It wasn't about a cause you could capture
with
all of those virtues and positive words.

It wasn't a cause you could podcast.

It wasn't a cause you could post.

It was simply a street corner,
folding me home...

folding me home to a place I don't own.

It was simply a flicker that lingered inside,
back when the world was a strobe light...

back when the beam simply pushed me aside.

It was simply a heart made of river and rain,
slipping through teardrops
and fingers...

precious when we crave it in the night-time,
sidelined
by the headlines every day.

It was simply a thing they call kindness,
with all of the righteousness filtered right out.

It was simply a thing they call touching...

simply a thing much like love.

Simply a thing that batters on walls
and bleeds out on floors
and hides behind shadows and cities and doors.

Simply the world that I carry each day.

Simply a placard with nothing to say.

Simply those lights at the foot of the sky,

stuck in the hope they make windows and doors for,

gliding through places that still make us cry.